The **Machu Picchu Historical Sanctuary** was created by Presidential Decree in January of 1981, as an area of 32,592 hectares to form part of the National System of Conservation Units (now the National System of Natural Areas Protected by the State) under the administration of the Ministry of Agriculture, "in coordination with" (details unspecified) the Ministry of Education—referring to the National Institute of Culture, which is responsible for the conservation of archaeological sites. After numerous bureaucratic changes in the ensuing years, the agency inside the Ministry of Agriculture now managing the Sanctuary is the National Institute of Natural Resources (INRENA). The founding decree declares the territory of the Sanctuary, in formal Spanish, to be "intangible," "imprescriptible," and "inalienable," meaning in essence that no part can be altered, sold or transferred.

Front cover: The sun's rays break through the clouds over Machu Picchu's urban sector. *J. Bartle*
Page 1: A view of the sanctuary from San Miguel Mountain. *J. Reinhard*
Page 2: Phuyupatamarca ("Cloud-level Town") is the highest settlement on the Inca Trail. The trail descends via a steep stairway, visible behind the ruins. *J. Bartle*
Page 3: The moon rises behind Salcantay (6,271 ms., 20,575 ft.), the sacred peak which dominates the Machu Picchu region. *B. Klepinger*
This page: A "Wiñay Wayna" ("Forever Young") orchid at the site of the same name. *T. Brian*
Opposite page: Morning clouds fill the Urubamba Valley below Phuyupatamarca, with the Wakay Willka (Veronica) massif in the distance. *J. Bartle*

Published by Nuevas Imágenes S.A.
Av. S. Antúnez de Mayolo 879
Lima 33, Perú
Tel.: (511) 448-8513
E-mail: jbartle@terra.com.pe

Impresión de 5,000 ejemplares en junio 2006
4a. reimpresión de la edición del año 2000
Hecho el Depósito Legal 2006-4923
Ley #26905—Biblioteca Nacional del Perú
Proyecto Editorial 11501400600361
ISBN 9972-9015-0-5

Printed in Peru

MACHU PICCHU HISTORICAL SANCTUARY

CUSCO, PERU

Peter Frost
with Daniel Blanco, Abel Rodríguez & Barry Walker

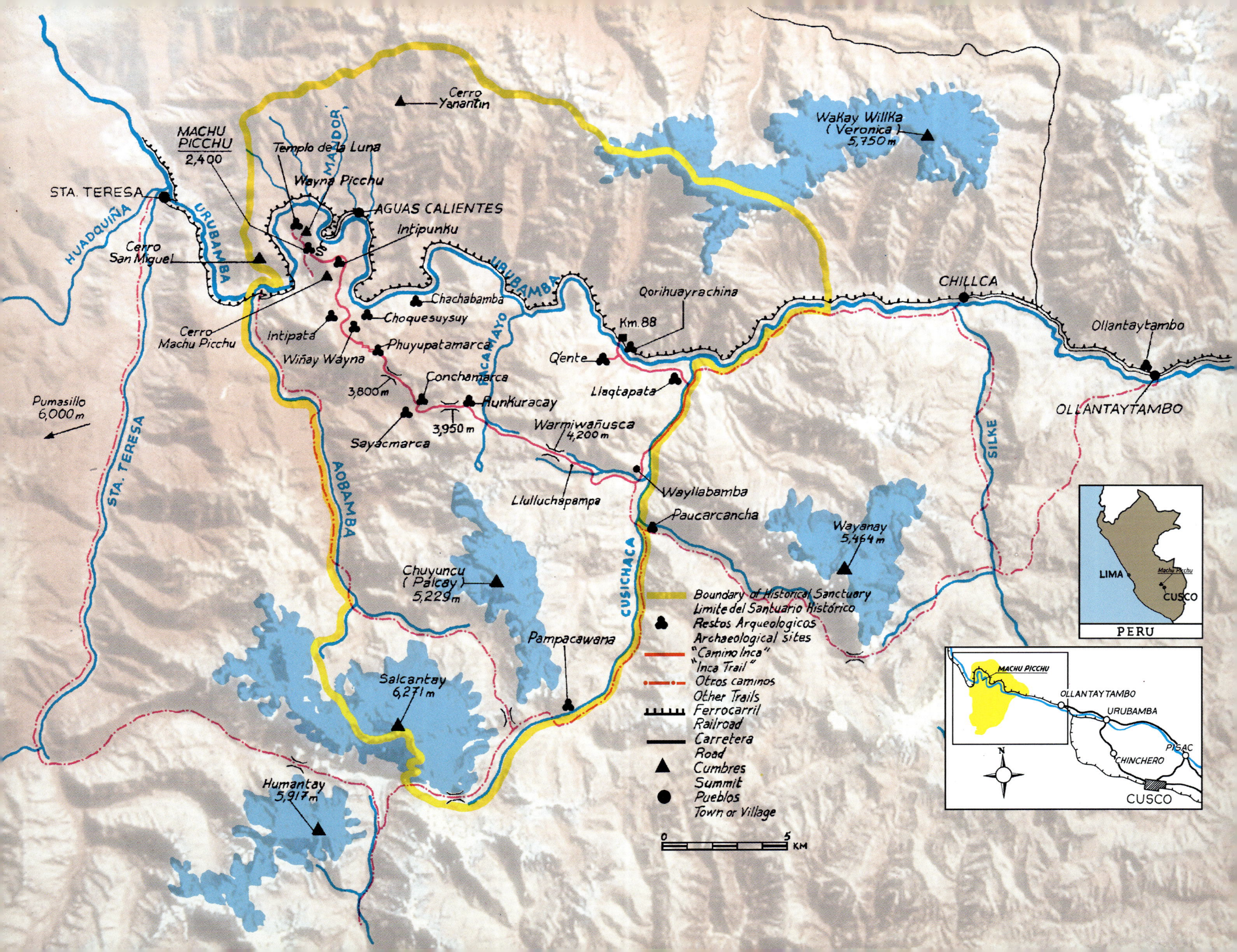

MACHU PICCHU
2,400
Templo de la Luna
MANDOR
Wayna Picchu
AGUAS CALIENTES
Intipunku
Cerro Yanantin
Wakay Willka (Veronica) 5,750 m
STA. TERESA
HUADQUIÑA
URUBAMBA
Cerro San Miguel
Cerro Machu Picchu
Chachabamba
Choquesuysuy
Intipata
Wiñay Wayna
Phuyupatamarca
3,800 m
Conchamarca
Runkuracay
3,950 m
Sayacmarca
Warmiwañusca
4,200 m
Llulluchapampa
Wayllabamba
Paucarcancha
Qorihuayrachina
Km. 88
Qente
Llaqtapata
CHILLCA
Ollantaytambo
OLLANTAYTAMBO
SILKE
Wayanay 5,464 m
Pumasillo 6,000 m
STA. TERESA
AOBAMBA
CUSICHACA
Chuyuncu (Palcay) 5,229 m
Pampacawana
Salcantay 6,271 m
Humantay 5,917 m
Boundary of Historical Sanctuary
Limite del Santuario Histórico
Restos Arqueologicos
Archaeological sites
"Camino Inca"
"Inca Trail"
Otros caminos
Other Trails
Ferrocarril
Railroad
Carretera
Road
Cumbres
Summit
Pueblos
Town or Village
0 5 KM
PERU
LIMA
Machu Picchu
CUSCO
MACHU PICCHU
OLLANTAYTAMBO
URUBAMBA
PISAC
CHINCHERO
CUSCO
N

29

Page 29 The ice-covered southeast ridge of Salcantay, the 6,271 ms. (20,575 ft.) peak which dominates the sanctuary, an area of astounding geographical and biological diversity. *J. Bartle* **Page 53** There are more than 370 known species of birds in the sanctuary, including these Andean torrent ducks. *T. Hendrickson* **Page 41** Wiñay Wayna is one of the most extensive settlements along the Inca Trail. It can be reached in two hours on foot from Machu Picchu. *J. Bartle*

53

41

CONTENTS

MAPS & SKETCHES

52

35

Page 52 Porters rest on the Inca Trail. Most porters come from traditional Andean villages along the Patacancha Valley above Ollantaytambo. *D. Blehert*

Page 35 There are at least 170 species of orchids within the sanctuary, including *Odontoglossum bicolor. A. Rodríguez*

Machu Picchu was not an isolated site, but the center of a large and populous Inca province spread over a region of spectacular geographic and biological diversity, ranging from dense tropical cloud forest to forbidding glacier-draped peaks. *T. Allain Chambi*

Lost Province of the Incas

Ever since it was revealed to the world early this century, Machu Picchu has evoked a fairy-tale image of a spectacular, orchid-draped ruin perched on a crag above a mighty gorge: remote; mysterious; alone.

An enchanting picture—but somewhat misleading. The discovery begun in 1911, and continuing to this day, was not of an isolated site but of an entire Inca province, abandoned to the forest. It was a region of elite settlements built in dramatic locations, with a very large proportion of fine ceremonial architecture. Machu Picchu was its center.

Today's visitors to the legendary ruins do not even see all of what was Machu Picchu itself; large areas of agricultural terracing and various satellite sites remain obscured beneath the forest, or lie beyond reach of the day visitor. Those who hike the breathtaking Inca trail see a little more of the Inca province. But to visit the region when it was alive and active, five hundred years ago, would have been to see a vast area of soaring, forest-covered mountains, studded with dramatically-placed settlements of white granite and frequently interrupted by large open tracts of agricultural terracing, corrals, granaries, small clusters of houses, and mountaintop observation platforms. Looking down from the heights into the precipitous gorge of the Urubamba River (the Willkamayu, or Sacred River, as it was then known), one would have seen meticulously-laid fields, green year-round with irrigated crops. And in all directions one would have seen runners, travelers and trains of llamas moving along the elaborate web of stone highways that held all this together: eight Inca roads converged at Machu Picchu.

The Inca sites of this region are extraordinarily well preserved, due to the quality of their engineering and construction, and also because the area was largely abandoned after—or even before—the Spanish conquest, so that these settlements were not subject to the systematic destruction that occurred elsewhere. We are very fortunate that today we can still admire a Inca region virtually intact, with all its superb quality of harmonious coexistence between humans and their environment.

This Inca province has now been recognized worldwide not only for its network of Inca highways and well-preserved archaeological sites, but also as a region of outstanding natural beauty and ecological variety, containing habitats for many rare plants and animals. It contains a startling sweep of altitudes and ecological zones in a small area, from the ice-capped 6,271 ms. (20,575 ft.) summit of Salcantay down through layers of high grassland and diverse cloud-forest habitats, to below 1,725 ms. (5,660 ft.) at the confluence of the Aobamba and Urubamba Rivers.

In 1981 the Peruvian government created the Machu Picchu Historical Sanctuary, an area of 325 sq. kms., for the long-term protection of this national treasure *(see p. 4)*. And in 1983 the Sanctuary was designated a World Heritage Site by UNESCO, one of only two sites in the western hemisphere recognized as both a Natural and Cultural Heritage Site (the other is Tikal, in Guatemala).

The immaculate care of Machu Picchu itself cloaks chronic problems of administration and conservation, problems which have today become urgent. Tourists are now returning to the Cusco region in unprecedented numbers after several years of decline. Their presence increases the flow of funds to authorities, but also add to already pressing conservation difficulties, which are virtually at crisis level.

Past attempts to address these problems have come to little, and the situation has only worsened. But a 1993 UNESCO-sponsored conference on conservation and management of the sanctuary has provided fresh inspiration, as many interested parties sat down to analyze the current situation and work out strategies for the future. The eighteen contributors to this book offer an overview of the Historical Sanctuary in the hope that future generations will still be able to enjoy and appreciate this irreplaceable cultural and natural treasure.

Superb construction remains well-preserved over long sections of the Inca Trail, which links an imposing series of Inca settlements before descending to Machu Picchu itself. Thousands walk the 43-Km. trail through the sanctuary each year. *H. Plenge*

The great Cusqueño photographer Martín Chambi took this view of Machu Picchu around 1920. Vegetation had almost covered the ruins again, in the few short years since they were cleared by Bingham's expedition. When Bingham arrived in 1911 there were huge trees and an even denser forest covering. *Martín Chambi*

Eighty Years of Exploration

Did Hiram Bingham really discover Machu Picchu that day in July, 1911?

Today it is fashionable to say he didn't. But it depends what you mean by "discover." As early as 1562 the Spanish recorded the existence of a district they called "Picho" (Picchu). Two other documents of the 1560s also mention Picchu. Somehow the Augustinian religious order acquired the lands, because in 1657 they "rented the lands of Machu Picchu." Machu Picchu and Wayna Picchu are both mentioned in two successive land transactions of 1776 and 1782. In 1865 the name Machu Picchu appeared on a map prepared by the Italian explorer Antonio Raimondi, and ten years later a Frenchman, Charles Wiener, mentions rumors of ancient cities "at Huaynapicchu and Matcho Picchu." And local farmers were, after all, actually living at the ruins when Bingham found them.

Yet if the Spanish were aware of Machu Picchu as a major Inca settlement they never mentioned it, or visited it. If they had they surely would have looted it, and destroyed the principal shrines and temples as they did elsewhere. It is likely that the 16th-century Augustinian realtors were dealing with lands in the valley below, and were unaware of the Inca city five hundred meters above them. Likewise, Raimondi and Wiener never visited Machu Picchu. And the local residents of 1911 had no awareness of the extent or the importance of the site.

Who, then, "discovered" the lost city? What is undeniable is that Hiram Bingham revealed Machu Picchu to the world—and therefore is sometimes called the "scientific discoverer".

What kept Machu Picchu hidden from the world for so long? The most obvious factor was the area's remoteness. After establishing Pachacuti's province the Incas bypassed it with a new route through the Amaybamba Valley to the north. This road became the principal access to the silver mines of Vilcabamba and the coca and later coffee and sugarcane growing regions of La Convención during the colonial and republican eras. The middle Urubamba Gorge remained in tranquil isolation.

But in the early 1900s a mule-trail was blasted down the Urubamba Gorge, and it was this trail which Hiram Bingham took in his search for the lost cities of Vilcabamba. At a place called Mandorpampa, he met a local campesino named Melchor Arteaga, who claimed there were fine Inca ruins high on the ridge above. On July 24th, 1911, Arteaga led a perspiring and skeptical Bingham to a place where two native families had cleared a few abandoned Inca terraces. Not expecting much, Bingham penetrated the dense forest beyond these terraces and promptly bumped into "one of the finest examples of masonry I had ever seen." Hiram Bingham's narrative of his explorations erupts at this point with exclamations like "spellbound," "took my breath away," and "could scarcely believe my senses." This is hardly surprising, since he had just made one of the most important finds in the history of archaeology.

Exploration was Hiram Bingham's great passion, at least during this period of his life (later it became politics). He was from an influential Yankee family, and attended Yale University, whence he first arrived in the Andes in 1909 to conduct research for a doctoral thesis on the routes used by Simón Bolívar in the campaigns of independence. During that journey he became intensely interested in the archaeology of Peru, and in particular the location of the lost city of Vilcabamba. He persuaded several colleagues to help him search for these ruins, and obtained financial support from the National Geographic Society.

Bingham called this sculpted cave below the Sun Temple the "Royal Tomb," although no human remains were found there. It contains some of Machu Picchu's finest stonework. *T. Brian*

He returned to Machu Picchu in 1912, the year after his spectacular find, to clear and excavate the ruins, and again in 1915, to conduct further explorations. During this period he discovered all the major ruins of the Inca trail with the exception of Wiñay Wayna. He also located the ruins of Vitcos, an important center in the rebel Inca state of Vilcabamba, and Espíritu Pampa, which he dismissed as unimportant. (If he had poked around deeper in the jungle there he would have realized he had actually found what he was looking for all along: Vilcabamba the Old.)

After 1915 Bingham published a great deal about his explorations, but did not return to Machu Picchu until 1948, when he came to inaugurate the new Hiram Bingham Highway which had been built from the river to the ruins.

Meanwhile access improved with the construction of the railroad down the Urubamba Valley from Cusco. Initiated in 1913, construction had proceeded by stages, reaching Aguas Calientes (Km. 110.5) in 1928, and Puente Ruinas (Km. 112) that same year of 1948. Today it reaches all the way to Quillabamba (Km. 172).

In the interim the Wenner Gren Scientific Expedition of 1941 led by Paul Fejos and accompanied by the famous Peruvian archaeologist Julio C. Tello had carried out surveys and mapping along the Inca trail, and discovered the ruins of Wiñay Wayna, the third largest settlement of the region, after Llaqtapata and Machu Picchu itself.

Recent Discoveries

In the 1980s Cusco archaeologists Wilfredo Yépez, Rubén Orellana, Alfredo Valencia and Fernando Astete, and the U.S. anthropologist Johan Reinhard, among others, have made many new discoveries. Among them: the major road and stairway between Phuyupatamarca and Wiñay Wayna; two new sites near Machu Picchu, close to the Inca trail, which have been named Killapata and Ch'askapata; an agricultural area, a quarry, and a huge combination wall/stairway/aqueduct at Mandorpampa on the north bank of the river facing Machu Picchu; a ceremonial platform on the tip of San Miguel ridge; and a road from the center of Machu Picchu down to a site near the hydroelectric plant at Km. 121.

Are there yet more ruins to be discovered in the Machu Picchu region? Possibly. The Aobamba watershed and the densely forested northern tip of the Wakay Willka ridge are the least explored areas, and could still produce new finds. In the meantime Cusco's archaeologists have their hands full studying and preserving the sites already discovered.

This puzzling opening in the Temple of the Sun, resembling an entranceway but leading nowhere, is similar to a doorway in the Qoricancha of Cusco. It has been suggested that the holes once held precious stones, but no one really knows. *B. Klepinger*

A: The Torreón, or Sun Temple, was Bingham's first major discovery. *B. Klepinger* **B:** In the early 1980s archaeo-astronomers discovered that a window of the Torreón was perfectly aligned to the sunrise point of the June solstice. On the morning of June 21, as seen here, a patch of sunlight within the temple is perfectly bisected by a line cut into the bedrock. Archaeologists speculate that the Incas used stone pegs set into the outer wall of the building to hang a shadow-casting rod for accurate observation of this event. *P. Frost*

A

B

An Inca origin myth mentions three caves from which the mythical founders of their civilization, the Ayar brothers, emerged. The Temple of Three Windows inspired Hiram Bingham to believe that he had found the origin-place of the Incas. But modern evidence suggests that the site was built and occupied by the 9th Inca, Pachacuti. The temple is one of the few examples of fine megalithic construction at Machu Picchu. It is also one of many open-fronted buildings at the site. The windows look down onto the central plaza and across the Urubamba Valley. Thousands of potshards were found on the terraces below these windows, probably the detritus of numerous religious ceremonies.
J. Reinhard, T. Allain Chambi

Orchids, bromeliads and begonias abound throughout the Sanctuary, although numbers have dwindled significantly at Machu Picchu itself—due to collection by visitors—and in other areas due to deforestation. *J. Bartle*

In 1989 archaeologists Johan Reinhard, Fernando Astete and Leoncio Vera discovered an Inca platform on San Miguel Mountain, with this view due east towards Machu Picchu, and to the mountain Wakay Willka (Veronica) beyond. Reinhard suggests that "the platform with its central stone was constructed as a marker of the equinox, as a place to worship this combination of mountaintop and sacred alignment, and for worship of the sacred geographical features on the horizon." For a wider view see page one. *J. Reinhard*

Mysteries of the Sacred Center

Machu Picchu's most alluring characteristic is its impenetrable mystery; it raises so many questions yet reveals so few answers. What sort of people built this magnificent city and its string of auxiliary settlements in such remote, inaccessible places? Why were most of the human remains female? How did an entire Inca region's existence remain unknown for centuries? When was it abandoned?

Hiram Bingham thought he knew the one simple answer: Machu Picchu was in fact Vilcabamba the Old, the last refuge of the rebel Incas, led by Manco Inca and his successors, who defied the Spanish for forty years. Vilcabamba was the fortress capital of a rump state, invaded and burned by the conquistadors in 1572.

But Bingham was wrong—Machu Picchu was not Vilcabamba. Its true location has now been established at Espíritu Pampa, a site some 100 kms. west of Machu Picchu. Today's sanctuary was never part of the rebel Inca state, and probably was not even occupied by the Incas during the period of resistance. This leaves a large historical hole in our knowledge of the Incas.

A Spanish document of 1568, recently discovered by Dr. John H. Rowe, states that the lands of "Picho" (Picchu) formerly belonged to the Inca Yupanqui—i.e. Pachacuti, the initiator of the classical expansionist era of the Inca state. The same document mentions that the surviving natives were growing coca in the Urubamba Valley there. But there is no suggestion that the Spanish were aware of any major Inca settlement in the area.

We know that this region was probably uninhabited by humans before the Incas, since there is no hard evidence of any pre-Inca occupation at any of the major sites. Earlier peoples had apparently penetrated no farther than Llaqtapata, the large Inca site at the beginning of the Inca Trail, just inside the modern sanctuary, which was serially occupied by several pre-Inca cultures.

So Machu Picchu was a planned Inca province—not an area that was populated gradually through periods of continuous occupation, but a string of new settlements conceived when the Incas penetrated into this region in the early years of their expansion (around 1450), linked to the highlands by a roadway of truly royal proportions and construction, and centered around a superb city.

There is no doubt that Machu Picchu was built by the Incas—although some still dispute it, claiming pre-Inca or even extraterrestrial construction. The architectural style of Machu Picchu is classical Inca, from the period of the culture's apogee, the mid-15th to early-16th centuries. In fact, if you would like to imagine what Inca Cusco looked like, Machu Picchu will do nicely as a model. Though the geographical location is very different, there are many similarities: one half of the settlement is agricultural, the other half is urban; the urban sector was itself divided into two parts; the streets were very narrow and the thatched roofs of the buildings were very steep-pitched; a moat (or river, in Cusco's case) divided the agricultural and architectural halves; and there were many cultivated terraces within the urban sector.

We know that this region was in some way special to the Incas, inhabited by some kind of elite group. This is confirmed by the superb quality of so much of its construction, and the high proportion of ceremonial types of architecture, particularly at Machu Picchu itself.

The Incas were a profoundly spiritual people. Unseen forces ruled their world, and they spent much time in different forms of worship, which were often related to the

The agricultural sector, with the "watchman's hut" at top, and the terrace workers' houses at left. In the background stands Machu Picchu mountain. *H. Plenge*

The Intiwatana is a superb sculpture carved from the living rock, at the highest point within Machu Picchu's center. Johan Reinhard notes that it stands at the crossing point of a straight north-south line between the peaks of Wayna Picchu and Salcantay, and the East-West line between Wakay Willka and San Miguel.
B. Klepinger

agricultural cycle or to veneration of landscape features such as mountains, rivers, rocks and springs. These were considered to be deities with whom humans could communicate, and who could bestow favor or visit disaster on people within their sphere of influence. It seems that the Incas considered Machu Picchu an important "power spot," a place where sacred forces were intensely concentrated. One very early Spanish document (written in 1565) may have been hinting at this when it briefly but intriguingly describes "Picho" as "the land of Peace."

The reportedly high proportion of females among the human remains found by Bingham inspired a popular legend that after the Spanish conquest this place became the last refuge of the Virgins of the Sun, the Inca caste of chosen women who were kept in seclusion. There was also a much older story, current around the time of the Spanish conquest of Peru, that the Incas had somewhere a "University of Idolatry", where their religion was studied, and its priesthood trained. At the time this was thought to be in Vilcabamba, which the Spanish later invaded. But it is quite possible that they had got the wrong location for a place that really existed, and that the "University" was actually Machu Picchu.

Whether or not this identification is correct, Machu Picchu is certainly filled with relics of the Inca religion. It has proved to be the perfect place for archaeologists to compare references from documents and chronicles of the Spanish colonial era with evidence existing "on the ground," since it is the only Inca site to be spared the systematic destruction that the Spanish practiced everywhere else.

Over the last fifteen years archaeologists have discovered many architectural and natural features that point to solstice, equinox, and certain star alignments, and the various sacred mountains on the horizon. A prominent example is the structure known as the Torreón—studied in 1981 by US archaeo-astronomers David Dearborn and Raymond White—which has a window and an "altar" stone, aligned within two arc-minutes of the compass to the June solstice sunrise (as precise as you can possibly get with the naked eye, which of course is all the Incas had to work with).

American anthropologist Johan Reinhard goes further. Placing the city in the context of his wide-ranging studies of pre-Columbian sacred geography, Reinhard describes Machu Picchu as "a cosmological, hydrological and sacred geographical center for the region" and as "a ceremonial center, where economic, political and religious factors combined to lead to its construction in one of the most rugged areas of Peru."

Reinhard notes Machu Picchu's connection to the Inca heartland via the sacred Urubamba River, and its relationship to various sacred peaks of the surrounding area. Salcantay (6,271 ms., 20,574 ft.) is the major peak of the region, which can be seen from various points on the Inca Trail, and from the summit of Wayna Picchu. As Reinhard emphasizes, Machu Picchu is connected directly to Salcantay, since it is built on a long ridge which extends from this great mountain all the way to the city.

There are so many other examples of sacred geography in the region that it has been described by archaeologist Margaret MacLean as "an encoded landscape." The sacred geographic features of the area are described in some detail in Reinhard's book *Machu Picchu: The Sacred Center* *(**see Further Reading, p. 61**).*

Another curious and related feature of Machu Picchu is the phenomenon of "echo stones." There are many standing stones, both large and small, both natural and carved, that appear to be miniature models of some peak on the surrounding landscape or, in one case, of a constellation—the Southern Cross. The exactness of these representations

A 1925 view of the Intiwatana, the so-called "Hitching Post of the Sun." According to Cusco legend, the Incas would ritually "tie" the sun to pillars like this one on the winter solstice to bring the sun back. However, modern studies suggest it may have been related to observation of the equinox. It may also have been a symbolic representation of Wayna Picchu. *Martín Chambi*

The Sacred Rock has been described as an "echo" of the horizon behind it. Interestingly it also echoes somewhat more exactly the shape of Pumasillo, the snow peak which lies in the opposite direction, on the far horizon. There are other echo-stones which seem to represent Wayna Picchu, the Southern Cross and other prominent natural features. *J. Bartle*

varies considerably, and some argue that they don't exist at all; they are just stones, and our imaginations have invented the echo. Yet they seem too numerous and suggestive to be ignored.

Besides the sacred character of Machu Picchu, the area must have had more mundane and practical functions. The center itself must have served as an Inca provincial capital and outpost on the fringes of the tropical forest, high and cool enough to be agreeable to the highland-dwelling Incas, yet close to the source of a vital crop: coca. This tropical shrub could be grown in the valley below Machu Picchu. The Andean peoples of that era chewed coca leaves (and their descendants still do today), and a steady supply was of vital interest to the Inca state.

Other products were important, too. The nobility wore clothes made from the skins and colorful feathers of creatures from the rainforest, and ate its fruits. Their healers used the forest's medicinal plants. In the days when this was a thriving Inca province the highway now called the Inca Trail must have been busy with trains of llamas moving these forest products up to the highlands, and bringing highland produce such as potatoes, beans and quinoa down to the people at Machu Picchu.

The extensive agricultural terraces of the sanctuary probably grew maize for local consumption and for burning in religious sacrifices, which the Incas offered in vast quantities. The same 1568 document which mentions that the lands formerly belonged to the personal estate of the Inca Pachacuti, states that the Indians formerly used the produce of this region for sacrifices.

But if the inhabitants were really sacrificing a large percentage of their crops, they must have been heavily supplied with food from other areas. As generously as we estimate production at Machu Picchu and vicinity (Cusco archaeologists Alfredo Valencia and Arminda Gibaja calculate it at about 28 metric tons of maize per year, assuming only maize was cultivated), the figures do not add up to a great abundance of food.

The permanent population of the center—judging from the number of residential structures—was between one and two thousand people. If each inhabitant needed, say, 1/4 kg. of maize per day, the 28 ton figure gives us food for only just over 300 people. Even if production were twice that, they still fed only 600 people. And if these figures are correct, they show that Machu Picchu was not self-sufficient even if the inhabitants were not sacrificing crops. It is probable that surplus food production from the agricultural center of Llaqtapata, near what is now Km. 88, was used to supplement the diet of the population at Machu Picchu. And perhaps scarcity of food was the reason why, according to Dr. George F. Eaton, Hiram Bingham's osteologist, most of the individuals found in burials died between 31 and 35 years of age.

Dr. Eaton studied the 164 skeletal remains found and reported 102 adult females, 22 adult males, 7 young females and 4 young males. The rest were infants, or unidentified. The 75% proportion of females inspired the legend of Machu Picchu as Last Refuge of the Inca chosen women. But many people have wondered since then if the identifications were really correct. Then in the 1980s the Peabody Museum at Yale re-studied the skeletal remains using modern techniques not availabe to Dr. Eaton, and confirmed the sceptics' suspicions: the true male/female ratio was roughly what would be expected in a normal population. The popular Virgins of the Sun theory recedes into the realm of folklore.

A

B

A: Hidden on the north slopes of Wayna Picchu, this structure within a cave is inexplicably known as the Temple of the Moon. It contains some of Machu Picchu's finest stonework, which bears some similarities to the (also misnamed) Royal Tomb. *T. Hendrickson*
B: The "Temple of the Moon" can only be reached via steep and dizzying Inca paths like this one, which leads around the west flank of Wayna Picchu. *T. Brian*

This Inca "drawbridge," a 20-minute walk from Machu Picchu, controlled access from the Aobamba Valley to the west. *T. Hendrickson*

One curious detail remains true: no skulls showed signs of cranial trepanation (holes cut in the skull). This surgical operation was usually performed on warriors with combat head injuries, and is extremely common in Inca burials elsewhere in the Cusco region. So we can assume that there were no warriors living at Machu Picchu.

Discoveries made since Bingham's time have roughly doubled the number of burials found. Even so, the small number of remains for a settlement this size suggests that the human occupation of Machu Picchu was fairly brief, and supports the currently-accepted theory that Machu Picchu was built sometime around the mid-15th century A.D., and abandoned about 80 years later. (Three paragraphs above revised from original printing.)

Machu Picchu was a continuous project, and many changes were made. Many parts of the city were under construction and unfinished. Indeed, it would only be remarkable if this were not the case, since any inhabited city has parts that are being built, altered or demolished.

One aspect of the city which would have been most striking at the time of its occupation but which has now almost entirely disappeared, is that most if not all the interior walls were plastered with baked, colored clay. Traces can still be seen in places, but the rainy forest climate has destroyed nearly all of it.

Trivia enthusiasts (Hiram Bingham apparently was one, since it was he who produced the following statistics) will be glad to learn that Machu Picchu has 109 staircases, with a total of 3,000 steps.

When was Machu Picchu abandoned? What happened to its people? As usual, we do not know. It is truly amazing that the Spanish conquistadors never heard about such a large and presumably wealthy prize, especially when we consider that so many Incas were collaborating with the invaders. How such an enormous secret was kept we shall never know.

There is general agreement that the region was deliberately abandoned, probably by a wholesale migration. The migrants must have taken their treasure with them, since very few precious objects have been discovered.

One theory proposes that Machu Picchu ran out of water. There are signs of unfinished canals, previously considered a failed attempt to increase the flow of water to the city. However recent studies by Wright Water Engineers revealed that these came from the same source as the other canals. In addition studies of the Quelccaya Ice Cap southeast of Cusco by Lonnie Thompson of the Ohio State University have determined that the climate in southern Peru was becoming wetter, not drier, during the early sixteenth century. Another theory attributes the evacuation to a fire which swept through the city. There is some archaeological evidence to support this hypothesis, but nothing conclusive.

The events which ended the Inca occupation of Machu Picchu may have occurred *before* the Spanish invasion. The Incas fought a terrible civil war lasting several years which was just ending as the Spanish arrived. There was also a great plague in the Inca empire around this time, probably a disease brought by the first Europeans. It may have been this period of slaughter and pestilence which depopulated the Inca province.

Another possibility is suggested by a Spanish document of 1562, which states that the rebel Incas of Vilcabamba "pillaged and burned all the Indian houses" of this area. They probably did this to create a "scorched-earth" zone between themselves and the Spaniards in Cusco, and to prevent the conquistadors from discovering and using the access routes to Vilcabamba from Machu Picchu.

We will probably never have final answers to the principal mysteries of Machu Picchu. That is one of the reasons it remains so fascinating.

A: The Temple of the Condor. The carved rock suggests the head and neck-ruff of a condor, while the natural rock behind may have represented the wings. Bingham called this sector the Prison Group, speculating that the underground passageways and the unusual-shaped niches here were used for punishment. *J. Reinhard* **B:** The Principal Temple has a massive "altar" stone. Its quality and central location indicate great ceremonial importance. Ground settling has caused severe sinking of the east side of the building. *J. Reinhard* **C:** The morning sun casts the outline of Wayna Picchu and "Wayna Picchu's claw" (left) onto the slopes of San Miguel Mountain. *J. Bartle*

B

A

C

The design of Machu Picchu is seen clearly from the summit of Wayna Picchu. The city was laid out along a narrow ridge 500 ms. above the Urubamba River. Its plan reflects the Inca cosmology of "complementary opposites," with the agricultural sector at top and the urban sector below. *W.M. Hern*

The urban sector is itself subdivided into two parts, with a large public square between them. The Hanan (Upper) and Hurin (Lower) halves of the city were probably occupied by different kinship groups. Most of the ceremonial architecture—including the Principal Temple, Temple of Three Windows, and the Intiwatana—stands in the Hanan part of the complex. *B. Klepinger*

An Andean condor *(Vultur gryphus)* soars in front of Pumasillo (6,000 ms.), a massif of the Cordillera Vilcabamba that pierces the skyline west of Machu Picchu. The Andean condor is the world's largest flying bird, with an adult wingspan of up to 3.5 meters. *T. Brian*

The Natural World of Machu Picchu

"In the variety of its charms and the power of its spell, I know of no place in the world which can compare with it. Not only has it great snow peaks looming above the clouds more than two miles overhead, gigantic precipices of many-colored granite rising sheer for thousands of feet above the foaming, glistening, roaring rapids; it has also, in striking contrast, orchids and tree ferns, the delectable beauty of luxurious vegetation, and the mysterious witchery of the jungle."

Thus wrote Hiram Bingham in *Lost City of the Incas*, his account of the discovery of Machu Picchu. Perhaps it was those same qualities Bingham describes that inspired the Inca Pachacuti to build Machu Picchu and its related settlements, and to create a kind of sanctuary-province.

Certainly those were the reasons for the creation of today's protected area surrounding Machu Picchu. The area bounded in the north by the watershed of the Wakay Willka (Veronica) massif, in the east and west by the Cusichaca and Aobamba Valleys, and in the south by the ridgeline of the Salcantay massif, encompasses a sweep of 4,546 vertical meters (14,910 ft.), from the 6,271-meter (20,574 ft.) summit of Salcantay to the mouth of the Aobamba River at 1,725 ms. (5,660 ft.)—a mere twenty kilometers away. This astounding plunge of terrain in an area of only 325.9 sq. kms. (80,543 acres) has created a correspondingly intense concentration of distinct ecological zones and habitats for a wealth of fauna and flora hard to find anywhere else on the planet. Andean condors soar above glaciers and grassy uplands above the treeline. An hour's stroll away, warm, humid air rising from the Amazon basin meets cool winds from the glaciers and forms dense and species-rich cloud forests. This compression of ecological layers is further intensified by the warm microclimate of the Urubamba Gorge, where species of flora and fauna exist well above their normal altitude range. The number of bird species recorded within the sanctuary adds up to an impressive 374—nearly 5% of the world's known avian species within a few square kilometers.

Scientists have classified the sanctuary into ten "life zones," ranging from the permanent snows of the high peaks through two types of high altitude grassland and seven zones of forest. The treeless mountain grassland environment known as the *puna* is familiar to users of the Inca Trail. This is the airy world of the black-chested buzzard eagle, aplomado falcon and mountain caracara, home to a large rodent, the Andean vizcacha, and to two of the sanctuary's three deer species. Although no longer present, in times past herds of vicuña and guanaco, the wild South American camelids, probably roamed here.

The best-known forest type in the region is the cloud forest, which includes four life zones. The most common type of cloud forest is characterized by a dense and varied mass of trees, draped in lichens, bromeliads and orchids and surrounded by bamboo and giant ferns. The sanctuary also harbors some of the few remaining native Andean *Polylepis* forests, which "hang" on the steep slopes and cliffs of the higher altitudes. These remnant forests support a high population of endemic bird species, many of them endangered.

There are many sub-types of forest within these life zones, such that the sanctuary supports at least 60 genera of orchid, with at least 170 species, some of these also in danger of extinction due to the impact of illegal orchid collecting and habitat destruction. Visitors may be lucky enough to catch a close-up sight of the native race of Peregrine falcon, mixed

Tropical cloud-forest vegetation clings to the steep walls of the Urubamba Gorge upriver from Machu Picchu. The warm microclimate of the gorge creates a unique habitat for many species of flora and fauna. *J. Bartle*

Looking across the Urubamba Gorge from Machu Picchu: Putucusi rises in the foreground, the pinnacle of Yanantin stands out against the horizon, with the Mandor Gorge to its left. The Santa Ana railroad line from Cusco to Quillabamba parallels the river far below. *H. Plenge*

A

B

flocks of dozens of colorful tanagers, or the Peruvian cock-of-the-rock (*p. 57*), which is something of a symbol of the sanctuary. The endangered Andean bear is still sighted within the sanctuary, as is the rare Andean deer, known as the *huemul*, or *taruca*; the commoner white-tailed deer, local cousin of the North-American Virginia white-tailed deer; and an extremely rare, seldom-seen pygmy deer known locally as the *pudú* or *sachacabra* (*p. 58*).

Relatively few species of reptiles have been recorded in the sanctuary, due principally to the inaccessibility of the forests. A rare species of poisonous snake, the velvet fer-de-lance, is endemic to Machu Picchu. Various snakes of the *Elapidæ* family and frogs of the genus *Atelopus* live in the forests above 2000 meters.

The Machu Picchu Historical Sanctuary lies on a geological formation more than 400 square kms. in area, known as the Vilcabamba batholith. This is a formation of intruded igneous rock, dating from the Permian (late Paleozoic) era, about 250 million years ago. The predominant rock is of varying types of granite, and virtually all of the Inca structures in the sanctuary were built from dressed blocks of this white or pale-grey stone.

At Machu Picchu itself geologists have identified granite, tonalite (quartziferous diorite), and a vein about ten meters thick of serpentine schist, the soft, dark green metamorphic rock which is much used to carve objects for sale to tourists in Machu Picchu and Cusco.

C

A: The remnant *Polylepis* forests above 3,500 ms. harbor many species of rare birds. *J. Bartle* **B:** The high grassland areas are known as "puna." The few people living at this altitude within the sanctuary graze sheep and cattle and grow potatoes. *J. Reinhard* **C:** A typical nocturnal frog *(Hyla leucophylata)* of the cloud forest. *W. Wust*

A

B

C

A: The Aobamba Valley, one of the sanctuary's remoter areas, descends from the glaciers of Salcantay. At about 3,500 ms. the high grassland gives way to cloud forest. *J. Reinhard* **B**: Many varieties of ferns abound in the dense cloud forest. *W. Wust* **C**: A well-camouflaged Emerald Toucanet *(Aulacorhynchus prasinus)* at a favorite fruiting tree. These birds often travel in pairs and can be seen in the lower altitudes of the sanctuary. *W. Wust*

A: The sanctuary contains thousands of hectares of habitat for the endangered Andean bear (*Tremarctus ornatus,* also known as the spectacled bear), which lives in high-altitude forest. It avoids contact with humans, and is rarely seen or photographed. Scientists worry that loss of habitat may threaten its survival inside the Sanctuary. *H. Plenge*
B: Numerous tributaries tumble through narrow ravines into the Urubamba River. Mandor Creek forms a spectacular waterfall deep in the cloud forest a short walk from Km. 115 on the railway line. *J. Bartle* **C**: The Urubamba River has a vertical drop of nearly one thousand meters during its 47-kilometer course through the sanctuary, creating spectacular whitewater rapids. Its waters also provide electricity to the entire Cusco region. *J. Bartle*

A

B

C

A

B

C

A: Known in quechua as "Wakanki" ("You'll cry"), *Masdevallia veitchiana* (10-14 cm.) grows in open sunny areas. Once abundant in the lower altitudes of the sanctuary, it has now been extracted nearly to extinction. (June-July) *B. Collantes* **B**: *Telipogon papilio* (4.5-5.5 cm. in diameter) grows below 2,700 meters in thick forest in cold wet areas among moss and lichens on branch. In extreme danger of extinction, the clearing of the Inca site of Intipata destroyed some of its prime habitat. (May-June) *B. Collantes* **C**: *Maxillaria floribunda* (each flower up to 3-4 cm.) grows at altitudes from 3,000 to 3,700 meters in open cold areas damp with moss. (July-November) *A. Rodríguez*

Orchids of Machu Picchu

In the Machu Picchu Historical Sanctuary there are estimated to be close to 300 species of orchids spread across the varied ecological niches in the terrain. This fascinating but little-known aspect raises even higher the interest in adventure travel and ecotourism. To the present around sixty genuses have been found in the sanctuary and more than 160 species have been identified and classified. However, due to the rugged nature of the geography only 35% or so of the territory has been studied; further investigation should reveal many more—and some unknown—species.

At least some species are in bloom throughout the year in ecological niches ranging from 1,725 ms. (5,660 ft.), the lowest point in the sanctuary, to approximately 4,500 ms. (14,750 ft.); the observant visitor will find orchids during any season. The best places to see orchids are in areas off the beaten track between 1,800 and 3,000 meters—that is, in the cloud forest. The best time is during the rainy season, between October and March.

The diversity of orchids is stunning. There are plants more than five meters high whose flower is more than eight centimeters long, such as the *Sobralia dichotoma*, and also one of the world's smallest orchids, a *Stelis* whose flower is barely two millimeters wide. Some are on the list of endangered orchids, such as the beautiful *Masdevallia veitchiana*, a once-prolific flower which has been virtually collected to death. Genuses include *Pleurothallis, Oncidium, Lycaste, Brassia, Stanhopea, Anguloa, Maxillaria, Phragmipedium, Encyclia* and *Odontoglossum*. There are more than thirty species of *Epidendrum*.

Among the greatest threats to the environment of the sanctuary are forest fires, which destroy valuable orchid gene banks and habitat, as well as alter and even destroy entire ecosystems. As it seems unlikely these fires will simply disappear, we should foresee the danger and search for viable options for the recuperation of the impacted zones in general, and for saving orchid species specifically. Nurseries with strict scientific standards should be established to conserve and propagate threatened species of orchids and other plants which can then be reintroduced to the forest. In addition these gardens could be used for commercial propagation in order to reduce the terrible depredation occurring today. Nurseries could save dozens of species (not just orchids) from disappearing from the sanctuary. They should in fact be located in different ecological niches—not simply in the most convenient sites—to include the greatest diversity of species possible. To take just one example, species of *Masdevallia* known for a long time in Machu Picchu such as *M. welschii, M. davisii* and *M. barleana* have been collected excessively for nearly a century. What will happen with other genuses?

The challenge is clear: to conserve the diversity of orchids in Machu Picchu. There is still time.

—Abel Rodríguez

The exquisite *Sobralia dichotoma* (8 cm. or more) is known as "Flor del Paraíso." The plant grows to more than five meters in height on open slopes of the cloud forest. (July-September) *B. Collantes*

A

B

C

The genus *Epidendrum* is one of the most representative in the Sanctuary, with an estimated thirty species. **A:** *Epidendrum secundum* (each flower 2 cm.) is known locally as Wiñay Wayna ("Forever Young"), and gave its name to an archaeological site. It is extremely common in many parts of Peru, with varieties in many colors. They grow up to altitudes of 3,000 meters in the sanctuary. (Year-round) *B. Collantes* **B:** The delicate and fragrant *Epidendrum ciliare L.* (6 cm.) grows on trees and rocks in the lowest altitudes of the Sanctuary. (May-June) *A. Rodríguez*
C: *Epidendrum sp.* (cada flor 3 cm.) *B. Collantes* **D:** *Epidendrum coronatum* (2 cm.) grows in open areas among other plants at altitudes of 2,800 to 3,200 meters. (October-December) *A. Rodríguez* **E:** Another variety of *Epidendrum secundum* (1.5 cm). *B. Collantes* **F:** An *Epidendrum sp.* found near Runkuruqay. *A. Rodríguez*

D

E

F

A

B

C

D

A: *Sobralia setigera* (8 cm.) grows in humid open areas from 2,000 to 2,500 meters. The flower is extremely delicate and blooms for just a single day. (December-April) *T. Hendrickson* **B:** *Altensteinia fimbriata* (individual flower 1 cm.) grows in open areas among other plants and has an extremely wide range, growing from 2,000 to 3,500 meters. (April-June) *B. Collantes* **C:** *Lycaste longipetala* (8-10 cm.) grows in open areas of the cloud forest from 2,300 to 2,800 meters. (November-March) *A. Rodríguez* **D:** The diminutive *Pleurothallis sp.* (1.5 cm) abounds in shady humid areas from 2,000 to 2,500 meters. *A. Rodríguez*

A

B

C

D

Of course orchids are not the only flowers in the sanctuary; there are many other distinctive species. Four examples: **A:** *Eccremoncarpus vargasianus* (6 cm.) winds over and around other plants in forest habitat above 3,500 meters. There are dozens of flowers on each vine. (May-June) *A. Rodríguez* **B:** *Cosmos peusedamifolius* (6 cm.), known locally as "panti," flowers on the ground in open areas from 2,500 to 3,500 meters. (October-May) *A. Rodríguez* **C:** Each branch of *Bomarea sanguinea* (4 cm.) can have up to forty flowers. It grows on other plants at altitudes of 3,000 to 3,400 meters. (October-December) *P. Frost* **D:** The extremely delicate *Metzelia* blooms for just a couple of days during the rainy season. It grows in poor soil from 2,000 to 3,000 meters. *A. Rodríguez*

A hiker pauses on the Inca Trail between Sayacmarca and Phuyupatamarca. *J. Bartle*

The Inca Trail—A Pilgrimage

The Incas built a network of at least 30,000 kilometers of main paved highways linking their principal population centers across what is now Peru, Ecuador and Bolivia, as well as parts of Chile and Argentina. These roads were tremendous feats of engineering, thrusting over snow-swept passes, through jungle canyons, and across scorching deserts, built with drainage channels and buttresses, stairways and tunnels, and so well constructed that large sections still survive despite centuries of neglect.

One of the best-known stretches of this imperial highway system remaining today is the route now known as the Inca Trail to Machu Picchu. It was among the most impressive of the Inca roads. Its finely-constructed settlements of shining white granite, set upon dizzying promontories over plunging, cloud-hung canyons, must have been even more breathtaking in Inca times than today.

Today the Inca Trail is a kind of pilgrimage for hikers from all over the world. Thousands of people take it every year, from independent backpackers, to one-day marathon runners (the record time from Km. 88 to Machu Picchu is six hours), to pampered day-pack dawdlers trailing armies of local porters, to parties of local students so poorly equipped it is a miracle they arrive at all.

The trail runs about 43 kms., beginning at Qoriwayrachina, better known as Km. 88 on the Cusco-Quillabamba railroad (*see map on p. 49*), although guided groups usually start from a feeder trail beginning at Chillca. The trail proper starts at the Inca town and terraces of Llaqtapata, a more or less utilitarian settlement which may have supplied food to the elite of Machu Picchu. From here the route climbs steadily up the Cusichaca Valley to the village of Huayllabamba, the last populated settlement on the trail. There it turns right, continuing to climb up the Llullucha Valley until it reaches the spectacular pass of Warmiwañusqa (Woman Died) at 4,200 ms. This first part of the trail was used as a smugglers' route by moonshiners in the 18th and 19th centuries, and the hooves of their mules destroyed the Inca paving. After Warmiwañusqa the trail drops steeply into the Pacamayo Valley, and beyond that the trail more resembles its original state, a road laid with slabs of white granite, climbing and falling across two more high passes, snaking through various ecological layers, before finally plunging 1,500 ms. down into the cloud forest at Machu Picchu.

The highway visits several ruins sites of exhilarating beauty, passes by Inca observation platforms and traveler's resting places, tunnels through two impassable cliff overhangs, and winds through some of the most beautiful mountain scenery in the world. Even the modern concrete visitor center, which sprouts between the sculpted terraces of Intipata and Wiñay Wayna like a moustache on the Mona Lisa, cannot spoil the breathtaking descent from Phuyupatamarca to Machu Picchu.

Walking this trail it is impossible to doubt that the entire experience was planned—there was nothing happenstance about the stunning combinations of scenic and man-made beauty. The Incas wanted those who walked this way to reel in awe as they crested the passes and rounded the corners. They designed the trail like a dramatic narrative, with a series of troughs, slow buildups and climaxes, each greater than the last, until the stunning finale, when travelers look down from Intipunku upon Machu Picchu, shining on its stone isthmus between two great peaks, far above the Urubamba River.

The Inca Trail and Machu Picchu are rarely, if ever, considered in this light, as an integrated work of art—perhaps because there is no work of art in our civilization on anything approaching this scale. And yet it can be argued that, rather like a Gothic cathedral, it *was* a work of art, with its intended purpose: to elevate the soul of the pilgrim on the way to Machu Picchu. Perhaps not all travelers on this highway were on a spiritual journey—some must have been menial laborers—but it seems likely that this highway was originally a pilgrim's route, its destination a sacred city.

Llaqtapata, near Kilometer 88 on the railroad line. The Inca Trail begins here, zigzagging as it ascends the Cusichaca Valley. *J. Reinhard*

A

A: The Waca (shrine) at Llaqtapata known as Pulpituyoq. Round structures are not common in Inca architecture. *J. Bartle* **B:** The site of Llaqtapata was designed for utilitarian purposes, in contrast to the elite sites further along the Inca Trail. The area probably supplied Machu Picchu with some of its food. *J. Bartle* **C:** The Llullucha creek rushes through the forest on the ascent to the first pass, Warmiwañusqa. This compact forest is unusual in the Andes. *H. Plenge*

B

C

A

B

C

A: Bromeliads and lichens drape the branches of a tree in the Llullucha ravine. *J. Bartle* **B**: Runkuraqay commands a view to the Warmiwañusqa pass and overlooks the Pacamayo Valley. It was a perfect site for observing the approaches to the Inca province, and also served as a *tambo*, a way-station for travelers and goods moving along the Inca Trail. *J. Reinhard* **C**: A string of porters nears the head of the second pass above Runkuraqay, with the peak of Wakay Willka (5,750 ms.) dominating the horizon across the Urubamba Valley. The Inca Trail is well-preserved from near Runkuraqay all the way to Machu Picchu. *P. Frost*

The ruins of Sayacmarca (Inaccessible Town) cling to a small spur below the second pass, overlooking the Aobamba Valley. Access is via a steep and narrow stairway branching off the main trail. *D. Blehert*

The settlement of Sayacmarca was tightly organized, but nevertheless allocated space for a large platform with a commanding view of the region to the west. *J. Bartle*

A

B

C

A: The first tunnel on the Inca Trail—4 kms. past Sayacmarca—is sixteen meters long, and was cut behind a huge leaning slab of rock. *T. Brian* **B:** The classic view of Phuyupatamarca, with its row of ritual fountains to the left. *J. Reinhard* **C:** Water still flows through the main fountain at Phuyupatamarca. All the major Inca ceremonial sites had these baths, which may have been used for ritual purification. *J. Bartle*

Phuyupatamarca was an important ceremonial site, enjoying this commanding view over the Urubamba Valley, and of the entire surrounding area. The red patch is the modern visitor center, and the construction along the river is the intake for the hydroelectric scheme. The final stretch of the Inca trail traverses the steep slopes of Machu Picchu mountain, at far left. *J. Reinhard*

A

B

C

A: Dawn's rays fall on the north face of Salcantay, seen from Phuyupatamarca. *T. Hendrickson* **B:** A white-tailed deer strolls tranquilly above Phuyupatamarca. *J. Bartle* **C:** A trekkers' campsite above Phuyupatamarca, with part of the Wakay Willka massif visible in the background. *J. Reinhard*

A

B

A: A spectacular 1,300-step staircase plunges through the cloud forest from Phuyupatamarca to Wiñay Wayna. This route was not discovered until the early 1980s. *J. Bartle* **B:** Heavily-laden porters race down the steep stairway, causing damage to the trail, according to some experts. *J. Bartle*

THE INCA TRAIL

Although only six kilometers from Machu Picchu, Wiñay Wayna was not discovered until 1942. It is the third largest settlement of the region after Machu Picchu and Llaqtapata. The nineteen ritual baths, some of them descending in the chain visible at upper right, actually outnumber those at Machu Picchu, emphasizing the religious character of the site. The ruin is perched on a spur above a deep ravine beside a stream cascading from Phuyupatamarca high above. *J. Bartle*

The semicircular building at upper left dominates the settlement, and appears to be associated with worship of the mountain Wakay Willka (Veronica). The site, along with its neighbor Intipata, was also partly devoted to agriculture; many levels of terracing remain hidden beneath the forest at Wiñay Wayna. *J. Bartle*

A

B

A: A family group poses in traditional finery before their stone hut in Huilloc. The weavings from this area are some of the finest in Peru. *D. Blehert* **B:** A porter plays an Andean melody on his *quena.* The haunting notes of this flute carry great distances in the clear air of the highlands. *D. Blehert* **C:** *H. Plenge*

C

A Heavy Burden

Many hikers on the Inca Trail use porters to carry their provisions and camping gear on this quite strenuous hike, which crosses three 4,000 meter-plus passes. Carrying 35 kilos or more, porters usually complete the entire knee-jarring descent from Phuyupatamarca to the train station in a few hours, a drop of some 1,900 ms. over 12 kms.

Most porters come from the villages of Huilloc and Patacancha in the highlands above Ollantaytambo. The Quechua people of this valley mainly herd alpacas and llamas and grow potatoes, which they trade for corn with their lowland neighbors. Their traditional ways are changing rapidly under the impact of a new road and the arrival of development agencies, as well as through their involvement with tourism.

A Birdwatcher's Paradise

The Machu Picchu Historical Sanctuary contains an impressive diversity of avifauna for such a compact area. This is due to the rapid succession of climatic zones in the Sanctuary. In Machu Picchu we find altitudes ranging from above 6,000 meters to 1,725 meters, from high puna grassland to humid subtropical cloud forest. Many bird species in the Andes have relatively small altitudinal ranges, and each habitat has species found in no other zone. Coupled with the microclimate created by the Urubamba Gorge, this creates great diversity—and a paradise for the birdwatcher.

As of 1995 approximately 375 species of birds are known in the sanctuary, of which around 200 can be readily observed while walking the Inca Trail. Without doubt further observations in remoter corners will add yet more species to this impressive list.

In the rain shadows of the intermontane valleys we find a dry climate characterized by short, scattered trees, shrubs and cacti. An early morning walk in this habitat, such as near Llaqtapata at the start of the Inca Trail, will reveal a variety of interesting birds. Partridge-like Andean Tinamous whistle from grassy fields and Torrent Ducks brave the whitewater of the rivers, swimming up the class five rapids, often accompanied in August by several improbable balls of fluff—their ducklings! White-capped Dippers bounce from rock to rock, searching underwater for crustaceans clinging to the boulders. Many species of Finches flit amidst the bushes and cacti, and Scarlet-fronted Parakeets wheel noisily overhead, easily visible with their bright green plumes, until they alight on a tree and seem to disappear, perfectly camouflaged in the foliage. Brightly-colored Hummingbirds compete for nectar where cacti and shrubs are flowering—Sparkling Violetears, Green-tailed Trainbearers, Bearded Mountaineers and the world's largest Hummingbird, the Giant Hummingbird. Be sure to get out early to see the birds, because there are few to see by 11:00 a.m., except for a brief pre-roosting flurry before dark.

Moving to higher altitudes we reach the bleak grasslands known as the puna. At dawn it is cold and as the sun rises it is easy to see many birds feeding as the temperature rises. Terrestrial Flycatchers known as Ground-tyrants fly from rock to rock in search of flying insects, and flocks of brightly-colored Yellow-finches spring out of the *ichu* grass as the shadow of a Mountain Caracara passes.

A short walk here will produce encounters with strangely named birds such as Cinclodes, Puna Ibis, Sierra-finches and Canasteros. Due to the abundance of diurnal rodents at this altitude (it is too cold for them to be nocturnal) there are many birds of prey, including the Puna Hawk, Cinereous Harrier, and Black-chested Buzzard-Eagle. Master of his environment, the Andean Condor soars majestically on wind currents, often traversing many miles without a single flap of his wings *(see p. 28)*. Despite its grandeur the Condor is strictly a carrion eater; it is incapable of grasping prey with its chicken-like feet.

On sheltered slopes, usually above 3,800 meters, grows *polylepis* woodland. This habitat is extremely endangered due to cutting for firewood, yet contains some of the world's rarest birds. These forests are usually isolated from other forest types and surrounded by puna grassland. Birds in this habitat include the White-browed Tit-spinetail, Tawny Tit-spinetail, Royal Cinclodes, Ash-breasted Tit-tyrant, Giant Conebill and an assortment of high-altitude Hummingbirds. Line-cheeked spinetails probe the mossy trunks and d'Orbigny's Chat-tyrants flit from tree to tree. *Polylepis* forest is hard to get to, but rewarding once reached.

But it is in the cloud forest that the birdlife reaches its greatest diversity. This is the forest

An Aplomado Falcon *(Falco femoralis)* checks that all is well before starting its next meal, a Greenish-yellow Finch *(Sicalis olivascens).* A ferocious hunter, this large falcon can be seen in open country within the sanctuary. *J.L. Venero*

found in the lower Urubamba Gorge (where not deforested) and the final two days of the Inca Trail. Here birds can be seen in mixed feeding flocks, as many as thirty species together. A morning of birdwatching in the misty cloud forest may produce many of the following: Cock-of-the-Rock, Brown Tinamou, White-rumped Hawk, Andean Guan, White-throated Quail-Dove, Andean Parakeet, Scaly-naped Parrot, Collared Inca, Violet-throated Starfrontlet, Great

A

B

C

D

A: One of the gems of the hummingbird family, a male Andean Hillstar *(Oreotrochilus estella)* rests between bouts of nectar feeding. This species will also hawk for small insects. *J.L. Venero* **B:** A showy hummingbird of the cloud forest, the Amethyst-throated Sunangel (*Heliangelus amethysticollis*) is very aggressive and defends its "trapline" of nectar-producing flowers from other hummingbirds. *B. Walker* **C:** The Green-tailed Trainbearer *(Lesbia nuna)* is a Hummingbird of open slopes and is strictly a nectar feeder. It can be seen buzzing around Machu Picchu on sunny days. *J.L. Venero* **D**: The Giant Hummingbird (*Patagona gigas*) is the largest hummingbird in the world. Unlike the majority of other Hummingbirds, this species spends much of its time hawking for insects. It can be readily seen near the ruins of Llaqtapata. *J.L. Venero*

Sapphirewing, Chestnut-breasted Coronet, Sapphire-vented Puffleg, Amethyst-throated Sunangel, Tyrian Metal-tail, Rufous-capped Thornbill, Golden-headed Quetzal, Crested Quetzal, Masked Trogon, Gray-breasted Mountain Toucan, Ocellated Piculet, Crimson-mantled Woodpecker, Crimson-bellied Woodpecker, Spot-crowned Woodcreeper, Azara's Spinetail, Marcapata Spinetail, Scribble-tailed Canastero, Pearled Treerunner, Streaked Tuftedcheek, Montane Foliage-gleaner, Buff-throated Treehunter, Variable Antshrike, Undulated Antpitta, Rufous Antpitta, Unicolored Tapaculo, Green and Black Fruiteater, Barred Fruiteater, Red-crested Cotinga, tyrannulets too numerous to list, flycatchers, tanagers, Green Jay, Mountain Wren, Inca Wren, Blue and White Swallow, Great Thrush, Andean Solitaire, Brown-capped Vireo, Dusky-green Oropendola, Mountain Cacique, Spectacled Redstart, and Slate-throated Redstart.

This is just a sample of the birds that may be seen in the cloud forest. The easiest time and place to see them is in the early morning along the railroad line between Puente Ruinas and Mandor, and along the rough trail half an hour's walk up the Mandor Gorge.

—*Barry Walker*

A: A soaring Mountain Caracara (*Phalcobaenus megalopterus*) takes advantage of the mountain updrafts. A member of the Falcon family, this bird is a scavenger and occupies the niche filled by crows in temperate latitudes. This is a common sight to hikers on the Inca Trail. *J.L. Venero* **B:** Bar-winged Cinclodes (*Cinclodes fuscus*). A member of the Funarid family of which there are 24 represented in the sanctuary. *J.L. Venero* **C:** A pair of Andean Geese (*Chloephaga melanoptera*) rest on the high puna grassland. These geese rarely descend below 3,800 meters and figure prominently in local folklore. The larger male is on the right. *B. Walker* **D:** The Stripe-headed Antpitta (*Grallaria andina*) is typical of the isolated patches of *polylepis* woodland. Not as shy as some of its cloud forest relatives, this bird may be seen in quite open areas. *B. Walker*

B

C

D

A

A: Two female Torrent Ducks (*Merganetta armata*) brave the currents of the Cusichaca River. Torrent ducks are one of the few species of waterfowl capable of swimming up whitewater rapids *(see also page 8)*. *T. Brian* **B:** The spectacular Lyre-tailed Nightjar (*Uropsalis lyra*) is strictly nocturnal but can be observed along the railway track between Aguas Calientes and Mandor in the early evening, hawking for moths. The female has a shorter tail. *D. Blanco* **C:** A lone Plum-crowned Parrot (*Pionus tumultuosus*) perched high in the misty cloud forest. Normally these parrots will be encountered in noisy flocks of up to twenty in the lower cloud forest. *B. Walker* **D:** Andean Guan (*Penelope montagnii*). Guans are members of the Gamebird family and feed on fruits and seeds in the cloud forest. They are under pressure in unprotected areas but remain common in the sanctuary. *B. Walker* **E:** A Red-crested Cotinga (*Ampelion rubrocristatus*) characteristically perches atop a bush in the cloud forest. This species can be seen up to treeline. *J.L. Venero*

B

C

D

E

A

B

C

D. Blanco (3)

A Feathered Dandy

The dazzling Cock-of the-rock is Peru's national bird, and virtually an emblem of the Machu Picchu Sanctuary. Its habitat is the cloud forest, from 2400 down to 1000 ms. altitude. In the sanctuary it can often be seen along the banks of the Urubamba River, from Aguas Calientes all the way to the hydroelectric plant at Km. 122 on the railroad.

The bird belongs to the cotinga family, and is quite large, the male being about 30 cms. in length (**C**). There are two species and four subspecies of this bird, the one seen at Machu Picchu being *Rupicola peruviana saturara*. The male's most famous characteristic, besides the brilliant bright-orange plumage, is its custom of gathering twice daily in groups of up to eighteen young studs at favorite locations, known to birders as *leks* (**A**). Here they screech and dance feverishly, in hopes of luring the shy, elusive and dull-colored female (**B**). There is a peak of *lekking* in September through December, but the Cock-of-the-rock hopes to mate all year round, spending an estimated five to six hours per day in these vigorous efforts to attract a choice partner. When one actually arrives the males become emotional and incredibly raucous.

Needless to say, this bird is not one of the species which mates for life.

—Daniel Blanco

A

B

A: The fire of '94 is thought to have been caused by a porters' campfire left burning at Phuyupatamarca, which stands directly above the rightmost plume of smoke in the picture. In dry years fire will travel at ground level through the underbrush in the normally humid cloud forest, breaking out in many separate places. *M. Murillo-SHMP* **B**: This shy and nocturnal *Pudú*, the Andean pygmy deer, was injured and driven into the open by the devastating forest fire of 1988. This fire was started by farmers clearing land for agriculture. *D. Blanco*

The Future of Machu Picchu

In the dry years of 1988 and 1994, visitors and residents alike stared in consternation at the smoke-darkened skies of Cusco, while the ashes of the Machu Picchu cloud forest rained from the sky. Fires burned out of control within the sanctuary (and throughout the highlands), destroying thousands of hectares of irreplaceable habitat for wildlife and plants.

At such moments the environmental crisis of the Machu Picchu sanctuary jumps sharply into focus, and the air is loud with public outcry. Then the fire is eventually put out, the rains come, and the blackened mountain slopes begin to turn green again. It is possible to believe that the cloud forest is returning. Apparently all is well. Most of the concerned voices fall silent, and the others go unheeded.

But all is *not* well. Man-made fires burn out of control every July and August in the Peruvian Andes; the '88 and '94 fires were simply larger than usual. These fires are not part of any natural cycle. They provoke gully erosion and landslides. They destroy wildlife habitat and untold numbers of rare plants, which are replaced afterwards by scrub and coarse grasses. It may take as long as two hundred years for cloud forest or *polylepis* woodland to regain its original state. If there is significant erosion or soil impoverishment in the aftermath of a fire, the woods will never return.

Fires are only the most visible of the conservation problems of the sanctuary. Damage from tourism both on the Inca Trail and at Machu Picchu, destruction of forest by encroaching farmers, illegal hunting and plant collecting, the pressure of burgeoning growth at the tourist town of Aguas Calientes—all these factors threaten the future of the sanctuary.

Understandably it is easier to ignore or deny the continuous deterioration of the sanctuary, or simply to shrug in despair, than it is to confront the gathering crisis. For to face the problems is to plunge into a thicket of conflicting interests and viewpoints as dense, thorny and diverse as the habitats the sanctuary was created to protect.

Proper management of the sanctuary has been intractably complicated ever since its creation in 1981. Eight public agencies—the National Cultural Institute (INC), the National Institute for Natural Resources (INRENA), the Regional Government, the Peru-UNESCO Commission (Copesco), the railroad corporation (ENAFER), the power company (ElectroSur), the Municipality of Machu Picchu Pueblo (Aguas Calientes), and the Ministry of Industry and Tourism (MITINCI)—plus a private hotel concession and a couple of dozen farming communities have some power to act autonomously inside the sanctuary. In addition the tourism industry, the inhabitants of Aguas Calientes and land-seeking farmers all exert pressure on management policy.

To delve any deeper into this jurisdictional tangle would leave space for little else in this book. But in essence, management boils down to a cumbersome form of power-sharing between the INC and INRENA. The latter, which manages the national parks system, is responsible for the natural environment, while the INC is in charge of the archaeological remains, including the Inca roads and extensive areas of terracing.

A highly positive step would be improved coordination between these two agencies. In fact there has been a move in this direction, with the signing of a management agreement between the two agencies in 1993. Another major advance would be the completion and implementation of the Master Plan, which has been under discussion for years. Both agencies need to have adequate and independent funding, which would for example allow INRENA to maintain a force of park rangers in the field. As presently constituted INRENA is clearly the poor relation of this family, collecting no revenues from sanctuary visitors, and its Cusco office (which does not even have a telephone) is located within an annex of the INC.

Local conventional wisdom holds that tourism is the main conservation problem in the sanctuary, and that the primary issue is damage to the archaeological sites. But others argue that even with the current level of funding and government attention, the Inca monuments can last hundreds more years, while with constant encroachment on the borders of the sanctuary, illegal (though unrestricted) animal and plant hunting, forest clearing, and most of all, the destruction caused by the human-made annual forest fires, the natural environment may not last very far into the next century.

From all directions, settlers have steadily eroded the sanctuary, clearing forest for crops and livestock, setting fires (the 1988 fire was started by farmers), and hunting a beleaguered animal population. Ten years ago the valley floor below San Miguel Ridge, in the very shadow of Machu Picchu, was a strip of forest. Today it is a banana plantation. Every year the primary forest in the Aobamba Valley is pushed farther back by illegal clearing. The tourism-generated population explosion of Aguas Calientes, near Machu Picchu, presses ever harder on the surrounding forest.

INRENA's Sanctuary staff has taken an important practical step towards controlling some of these problems with the completion in 1994 of a census of all private farm properties within the sanctuary, thus legally clarifying that, at least in theory, no further land encroachment can take place. Existing farmlands cannot be sold, or passed on for more than one generation, so that parts of the sanctuary should eventually revert to public ownership.

One difficulty for conservation lies in the way the sanctuary was originally drawn up. The principal eastern and western boundaries were drawn along the courses of the Cusichaca and Aobamba Rivers, placing one bank inside and one outside the sanctuary. Most ecologists would argue that the proper course would have been to place the entire watersheds of both rivers within the sanctuary. Future action could include the expansion of the sanctuary to include these areas.

Such action might brighten the outlook for the Andean bear (*Tremarctus ornatus*), the "flagship" animal species of the sanctuary. Unlike its prolific and fearless North American counterpart, the only South American bear is timid and highly endangered, both from hunting and from destruction of its habitat. Naturalists had hoped that the sanctuary would serve as one of the few places in the Andes where the bear could be effectively protected. But only about half the existing sanctuary is suitable bear habitat, and this is effectively subdivided into two entirely separate ranges by the impassable (to bears) torrent of the Urubamba River. Add to this the environmental pressures already mentioned, and the Andean bear's future even in this protected sanctuary seems in doubt.

Tourism certainly is also a significant environmental problem. The Inca Trail is subject to intense pressure: 14,480 hikers took the trail in 1993, and in 1994 the figure jumped 57% to 23,349. All those feet wear away the stones forming the trail. These visitors dump prodigious quantities of trash, and leave the landscape smeared with human waste and toilet paper. They light camp fires, using the forests for firewood, damaging ruins sites, and sometimes starting forest fires (the 1994 fire was probably started by an unextinguished porter's fire).

The ruins of Machu Picchu themselves pose a special problem. Fortunately the area is seismically stable, but the human equivalent of an earthquake arrives every day on the train from Cusco. Hundreds of pairs of feet wear away the stone walks and stairways. Careless hands dislodge stones from walls. And just the innocent weight of all these bodies helps to accelerate ground settling. More than 113,000 visitors came to Machu Picchu in 1993, and in 1994 the figure rose 63% to above 184,000—an average of more than 500 per day. Greater numbers are projected for future years.

In the area of the Principal Temple, the Torreón and the Intiwatana—three of the finest

A

B

A: At times hikers seem to overrun the Inca Trail. Garbage piles up at campsites and parts of the trail are being eroded. An effective management plan is sorely needed. *H. Plenge*
B: Aguas Calientes lies just 1.5 kms. upstream from the bridge over the Urubamba below Machu Picchu. Many visitors stay here, enjoying its hot springs, and its economy depends almost entirely on tourism. The population more than doubled between 1980 and 1992, creating ever greater pressures for development in the sanctuary. *J. Bartle*

A

B

A: The recent clearing of Intipata in valuable cloud forest habitat has renewed controversy over the proper manner to conserve the sanctuary. *H. Plenge* **B**: The intake for the hydroelectric scheme at Km. 107 on the railroad, with the Inca site of Choquesuysuy at top. The hydro project was built in the 1960s—before the official creation of the Historical Sanctuary—and supplies power to the entire region. The network of power lines and the outlets, located downstream beyond Machu Picchu, have seriously impacted the sanctuary. *J. Bartle*

structures of the site—settling caused by rainwater seepage and inadequate drainage is causing the Inca buildings to sag perilously. In fact the site was already suffering geological settling even while it was occupied by the Incas, as evidenced by stone wedges cunningly inserted in various terrace walls to adjust for subsidence. The absence of natural vegetation cover or crops and lack of maintenance on most of the terraces also threatens to provoke further serious erosion in future.

The temptation to accommodate Machu Picchu to the convenience of visitors has led to distortions and even outright remodelling of the ruins. In some cases the layout of the city has been altered to make tourist access easier. The most flagrant example is the place where visitors enter the city today. The stairway and the gap in the wall leading abruptly onto the terraces of the agricultural sector is not Inca. It dates from sometime during the decidedly post-Inca Cold War era.

All too often archaeological reconstruction has been done without any studies having been conducted first, which may account for some of the gaps in our knowledge of Machu Picchu. If some sites had been excavated before being reconstructed we would now have better information on the uses to which those areas were put. A reconstructed site is lost forever to archaeology. These ongoing problems can only be addressed when those in charge become more aware of them. This is happening to some degree, with the publication of books such as Alfredo Valencia and Arminda Gibaja's summary of the studies and reconstructions carried out at Machu Picchu.

The very concept of a sanctuary—a place of refuge where certain human activities are forbidden or strictly limited—is often hard to accept in a poor country with rapid population growth. Aside from the encroachment of farming, pressure for future tourism development is already immense and still growing. The municipal authorities of Aguas Calientes want to build new housing at Mandorpampa, at the foot of Wayna Picchu. They also want to blast a highway up the Cusichaca Valley to the community of Wayllabamba, which would effectively obliterate the first section of the Inca Trail. Since the nature of the sanctuary has never been adequately defined, these authorities believe they can act without restrictions.

The Inca province of Machu Picchu may be the world's finest historic example of advanced human culture in harmonious coexistence with nature; this "Tao" formed its very essence. Today it seems deeply ironic that it should be threatened with destruction by conflict between those same two forces. Ironic, but perhaps not surprising. The mind that created Machu Picchu worshipped nature. The European mind that arrived in 1532 considered its own culture to be the very work of God, and nature a force to be conquered and subdued.

A conference sponsored by UNESCO in 1993 provided some fresh hope for a modern reconciliation of these polarities, as many interested parties sat down together to work out conservation strategies for the future. According to these experts, the overall situation is critical. Yet Peru has a huge stake in protecting the Machu Picchu region for reasons of both economics and national identity. And perhaps seven million dollars earmarked for environmental-protection and sustainable development projects from a debt-for-nature swap financed by the Finnish government will bring some real progress. So there are grounds for cautious optimism; there is still hope for a well-managed and protected sanctuary.

Only two years after its creation, the Sanctuary was designated by UNESCO—at the request of the Peruvian government—as both a natural and a cultural World Heritage Site. This designation is far more than a mere garland, a point of national pride, or a potential source international funding. By joining more than one hundred nations in the Convention on World Heritage, Peru has declared to the international community that Machu Picchu is a treasure not just for the nation, but for humanity as a whole, and pledges to conserve it for the future. It is a serious commitment.

Further Reading

Lost City of the Incas—Hiram Bingham, Atheneum, New York, 1963. Famous account of his discovery.
Portrait of an Explorer—Alfred Bingham, Atheneum, New York, 1963. Biography of Hiram Bingham by his grandson.
The Conquest of the Incas—John Hemming, Harcourt, Brace, Jovanovich, London, 1970. The classic account of the fall of the Inca empire.
Monuments of the Incas—Edward Ranney, New York Graphic Society, New York, 1982. Beautiful black-and-white photographs of the best-known Inca structures, with text by John Hemming.
Machu Picchu: The Sacred Center—Johan Reinhard, Nuevas Imágenes, Lima, 1991. Theories and observations by a renowned Andean explorer and high-altitude archaeologist.
The Inka Empire and its Andean Origins—Craig Morris & Adriana von Hagen, Abbeville Press, New York, 1993. Excellent overview of pre-Columbian Peru.
Exploring Cusco—Peter Frost, Nuevas Imágenes, Lima, 1989. Guide to the Cusco region and Machu Picchu by the author of this book.
Sixpac Manco, Travels among the Incas—Vincent R. Lee, self-published, Wilson WY, 1985. Entertaining and informative account of the author's researches in the Vilcabamba region.

More academic and/or difficult to find

Inka Settlement Planning—John Hyslop, U. of Texas Press, Austin, 1990.
The Inka Road System—John Hyslop, Academic Press Inc., Orlando, 1984.
Inca Architecture—Louise Margolies & Graziano Gasparini, U. of Indiana, Bloomington, 1984.
Archaeological Exploration in the Cordillera Vilcabamba, Southeastern Peru—Paul Fejos, Viking Fund Publications in Anthropology #3, New York, 1944.
Sacred Water, Sacred Land: Inca Landscape Planning in the Cusco Area—Margaret MacLean, doctoral dissertation, U. of California, Berkeley, 1986.
Carving the World: Inca Monumental Sculpture and Landscape—Marten van de Guchte, doctoral dissertation, U. of Illinois, Urbana, 1990.

In Spanish

Machu Picchu, Devenir Histórico y Cultural—Efraín Chevarría H. (editor), Editorial Universitaria UNSAAC, Cusco, 1992.
Machu Picchu, Enigmática Ciudad Inka—Victor Angles V., Lima 1992.
De las Sacerdotisas, Brujas y Adivinas de Machu Picchu—Marino O. Sánchez Macedo, self-published, Cusco, 1989.
Machu Picchu: La Investigación y Conservación del Monumento Arqueológico después de Hiram Bingham—Alfredo Valencia Z. & Arminda Gibaja O., Municipalidad del Qosqo, Cusco, 1992.
Qosqo en Flor—Abel Rodríguez A., Municipalidad de Qosqo, Cusco, 1991.
Orquídeas del Perú—Moisés Cavero, Benjamín Collantes, César Patroni, Centro de Datos para la Conservación del Perú, Lima, 1991.
Arqueología del Santuario Histórico Nacional y Sitio Patrimonio Mundial de Machu Picchu: Estado de la Cuestión y Propuestas para un Plan Maestro—Elías Mujica et al., UNESCO, Lima, 1994.

A llama enjoys the early morning sun near the Watchman's Hut, Machu Picchu. *J. Bartle*

A storm approaches Machu Picchu from the Mandor Gorge. *H. Plenge*

Looking back from Phuyupatamarca toward Sayacmarca on the Inca Trail. The water- and rainbow-worshiping Incas found these elements in abundance in their rainy province. *D. Blehert*

Contributors

PETER FROST has written extensively on the Cusco region over the past twenty years and is the author of *Exploring Cusco*, the most popular guide to the region. He is also a guide for the adventure travel agency Wilderness Travel.

JIM BARTLE is director of Nuevas Imágenes, a publishier in Lima specializing in the natural and cultural wonders of Peru. He is the author of *Trails of the Cordilleras Blanca & Huayhuash* and *Parque Nacional Huascarán*, and co-author of *Cordillera Huayhuash*.

Teo Allaín Chambi is the cultural director for the Banco Wiese Sudameris in Cusco. He has ably continued the tradition of his granfather Martín Chambi in black and white photography.

Daniel Blanco is scientific director of the Association for the Conservation of the Southern Rainforest (ACSS). He is writing his masters thesis on the cock-of-the-rock.

David Blehert is an experienced adventure guide and photographer who has explored in more than twenty countries. He and his wife Deborah Koehn are owners of Hale Kai, an adventure travel agency in Hawaii.

Terry Brian is the owner of Earthquest in Arizona, and has worked as a trekking and river guide throughout South America for more than twenty years.

Martín Chambi (1891-1973) was one of the world`s first master photographers. His expressive black-and-0white photographs of life around Cusco in the first half of the century have been exhibited around the world and published in many books.

Benjamín Collantes is a biologist and co-author of *Orquideas del Perú*. He has photographed more than 600 species of orchids in Peru.

Tom Hendrickson is manageing director of Pan Andean Tours in Cusco and the Tambopata Lodge in Madre de Dios. He has explored in the Cusco region for more than twenty years.

Warren Martin Hern is a physician, epidemiologist and anthropologist who has worked for thirty years with the Shipibo people of the Peruvian Amazon. He is an accomplished photographer who has traveled extensively in Peru.

Bruce Klepinger runs Ibex Expeditions runs Ibex Expeditions, an adventure travel company based in Oregon. He has guided adventure and cultural traips in more than fifty countries for twenty-five years, and has compiled one of the world's best collections of travel photography.

Mario Murillo is a former executive director of the Machu Picchu Historical Sanctuary.

Heinz Plenge is Peru`s most accomplished nature photographer. His work has appeared in dozens of publications, including *National Geographic* and *Geo*. He is the author of *Peru: Vida Silvestre*, a book on wildlife in Peru.

Johan Reinhard is an anthropologist, resident explorer at the National Geographic Society, field associate of the Field Musem in Chicago, and visiting scholar at The Mountain Institute. He is the author of *The Nazca Lines: A New Perspective on their Origin and Meaning* and *Machu Picchu: The Sacred Center*. In 1995 he discovered "Juanita," a young girl sacrificed by the Incas, near the summit of the 6200m Ampato in southern Peru.

Abel Rodriguez is a former ranger of the Machu Picchu Historical Sanctuary. He is anexpert on the fora of the region, and author of *Qosqo en Flor*.

José Luis Venero is an ornithologist and professor of ecology at the Universidad Nacional San Antonio Abad del Cusco, and director of its Museum of Natural History.

Barry Walker is the manager of Manu Expeditions in Cusco, and a leading expert in ornithology in Peru.

Walter Wust is an ornithologist, write and photographer who has worked extensively in the Peruvian Amazon and other natural areas. He is the author of *Manu: The Last Refuge*.

In addition to the above, many other people made invaluable contributions, including Alfredo Ferreyros of Explorandes, Carlos Leiva, the staff of the Machu Picchu Historical Sanctuary, Freddy Padovani, Tony Luscombe, Germán Coronado, David Ricalde, Guisella Tesoro, Américo Rivas, David Bennett, Eleanor Griffis de Zuñida of the Peruvian Times, and Miguel Unger, Rocío Avila and Roberto Roig of Automas S.A. Special thanks to Julia Chambi for permission to reproduce the photographs of Martín Chambi.